THIS COLORING BOOK BELONGS TO:

_____

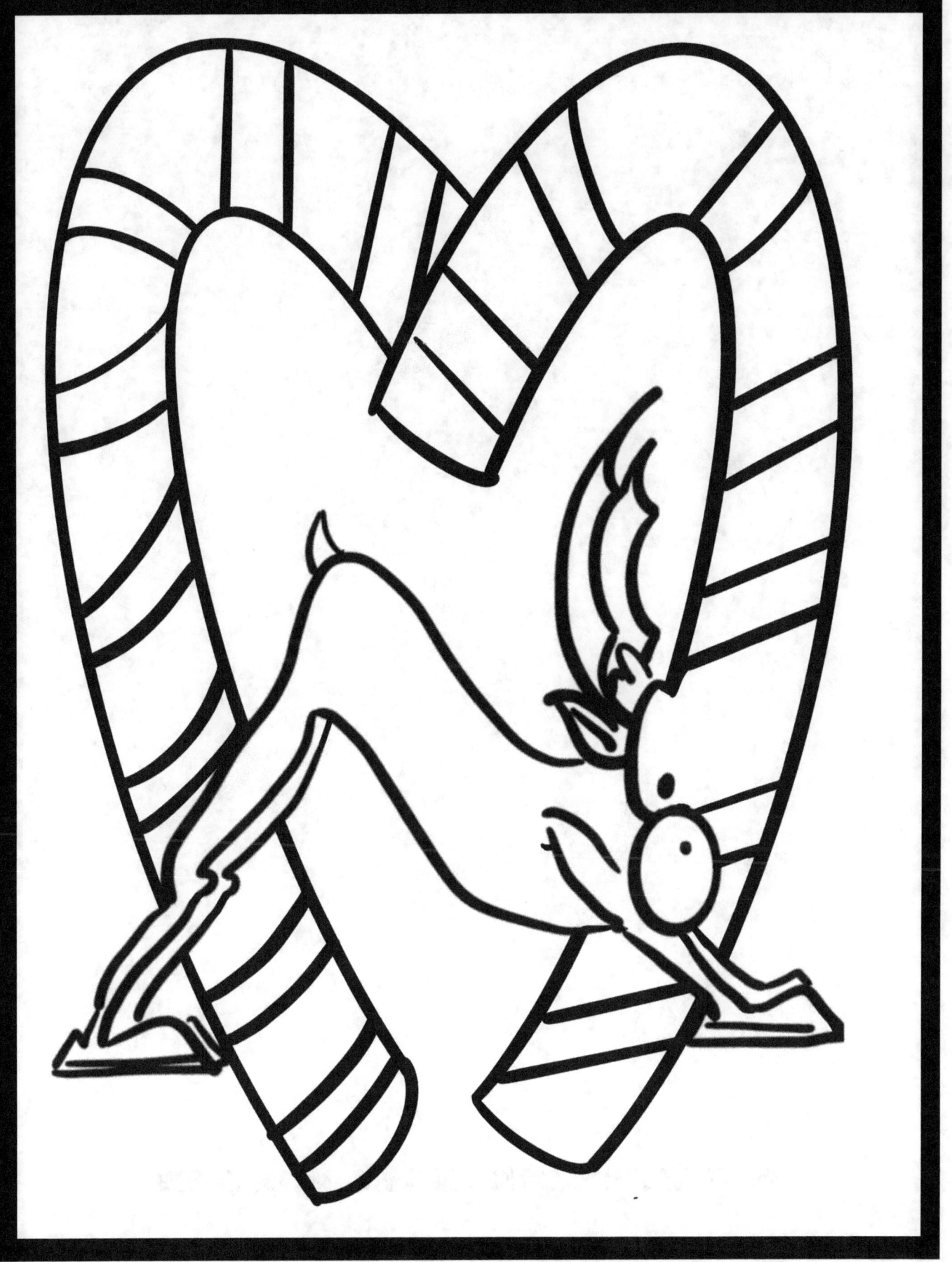

DOWNWARD FACING CANDY CANE REINDEER

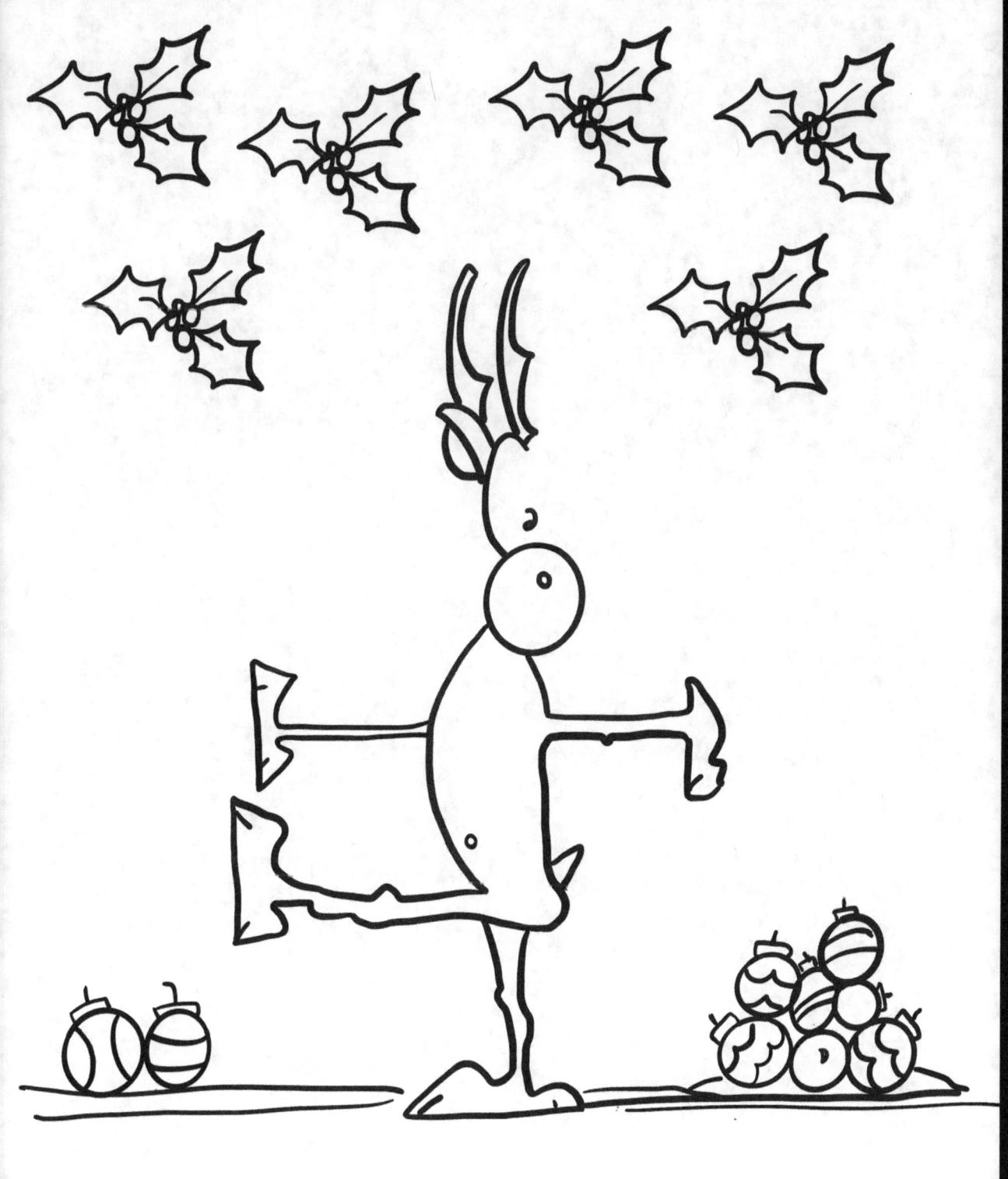

STANDING TWISTED REINDEER

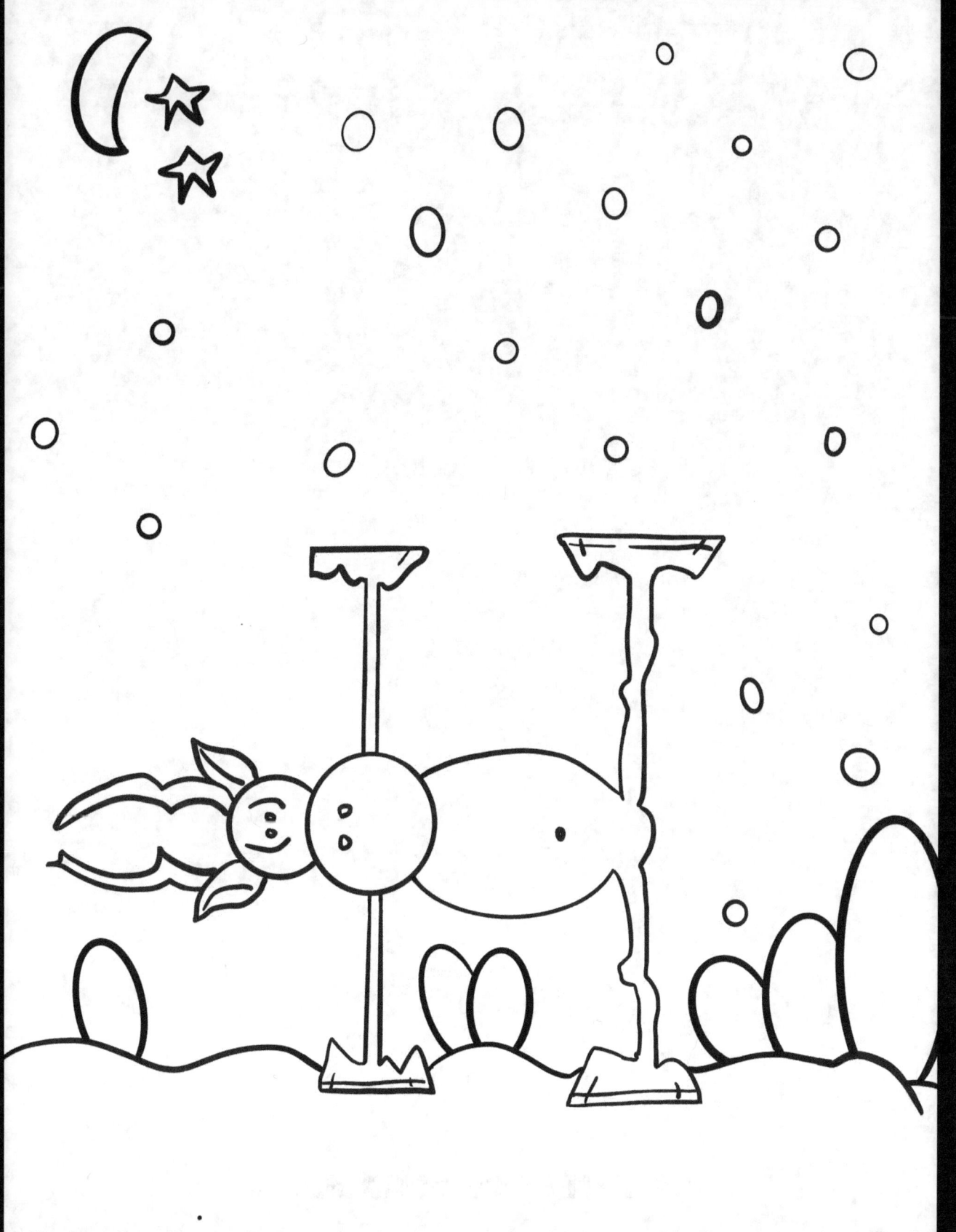

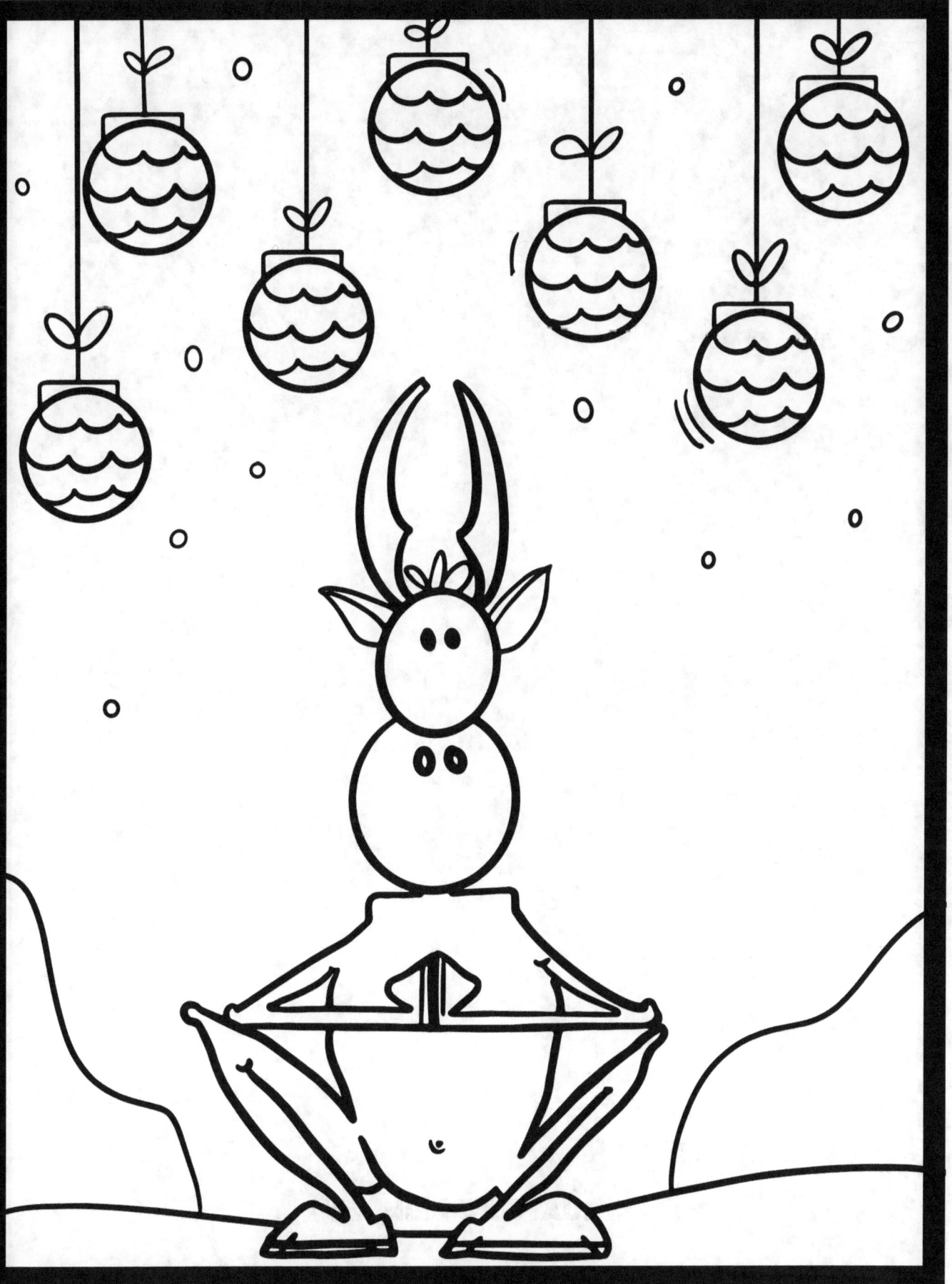

SQUATTING REINDEER

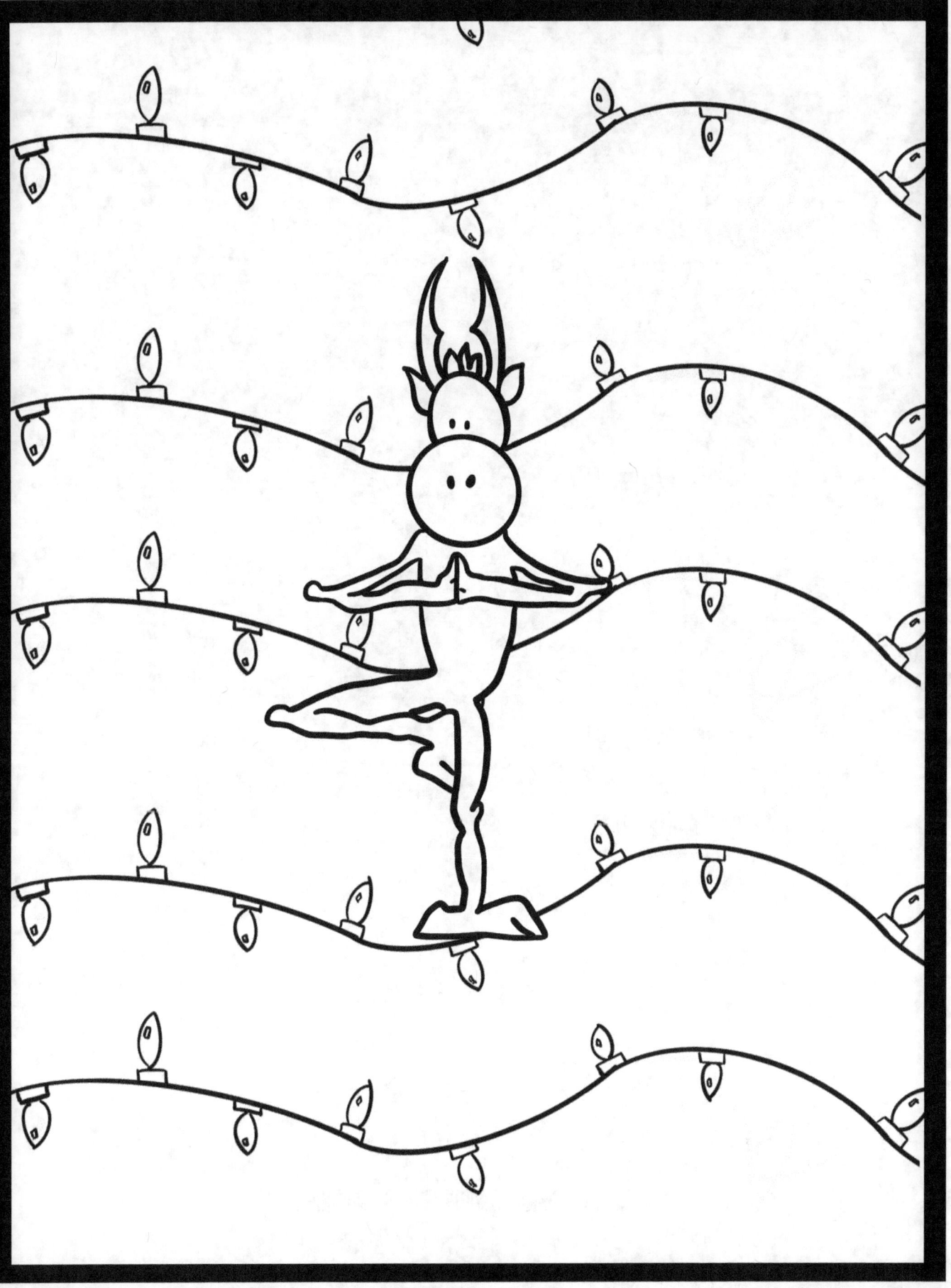

LIGHTED TREE REINDEER

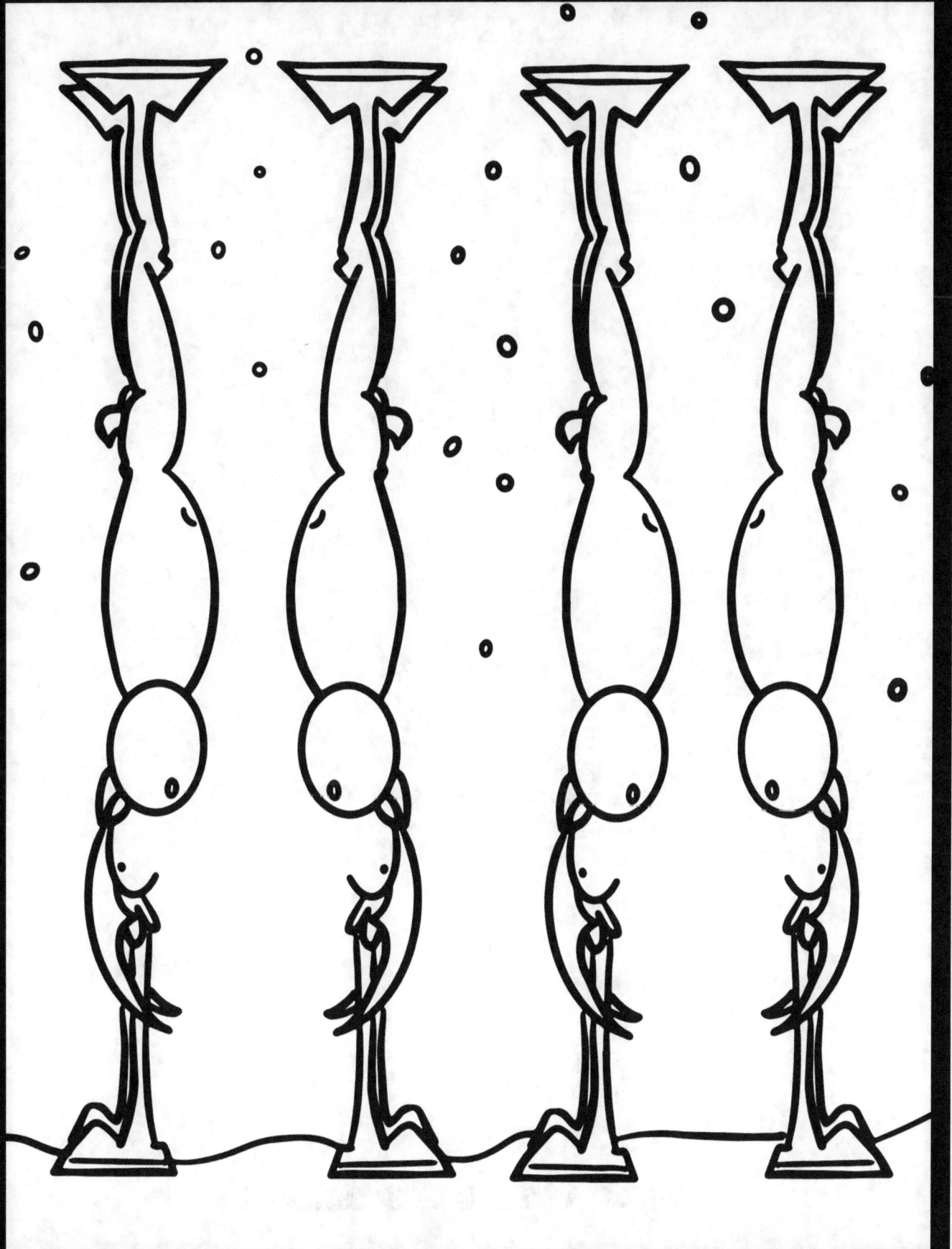

HANDSTAND REINDEER QUARTET

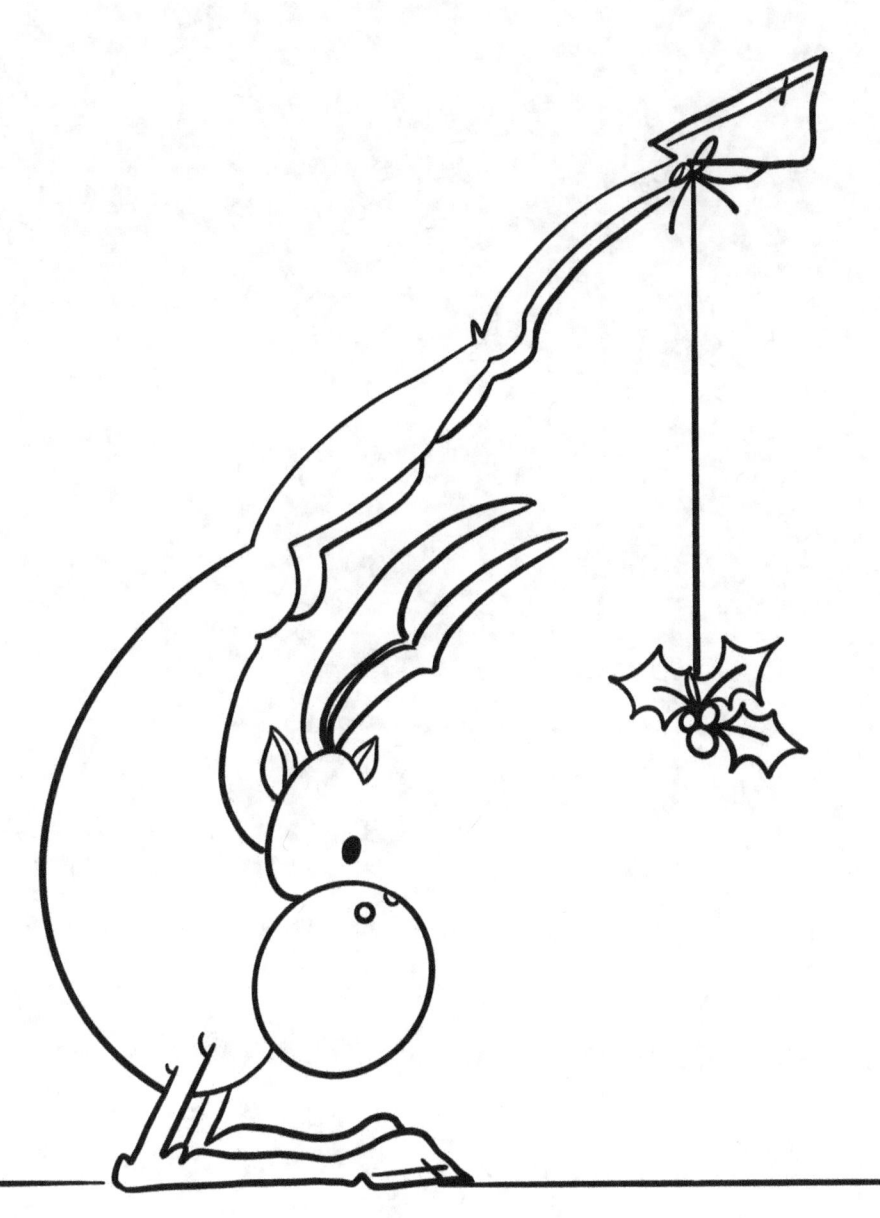

FOREARM STAND REINDEER

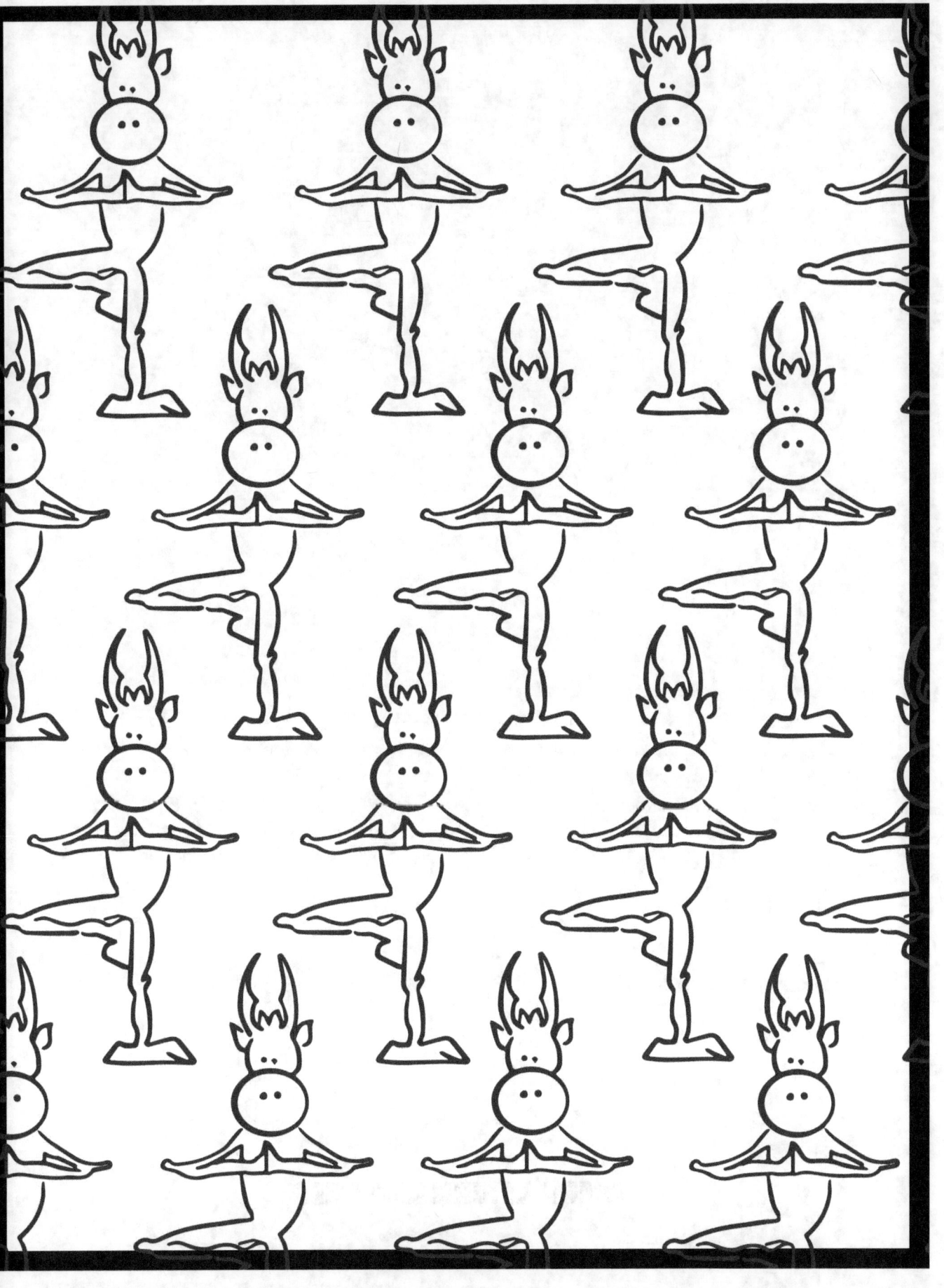

TREE PATTERN REINDEER

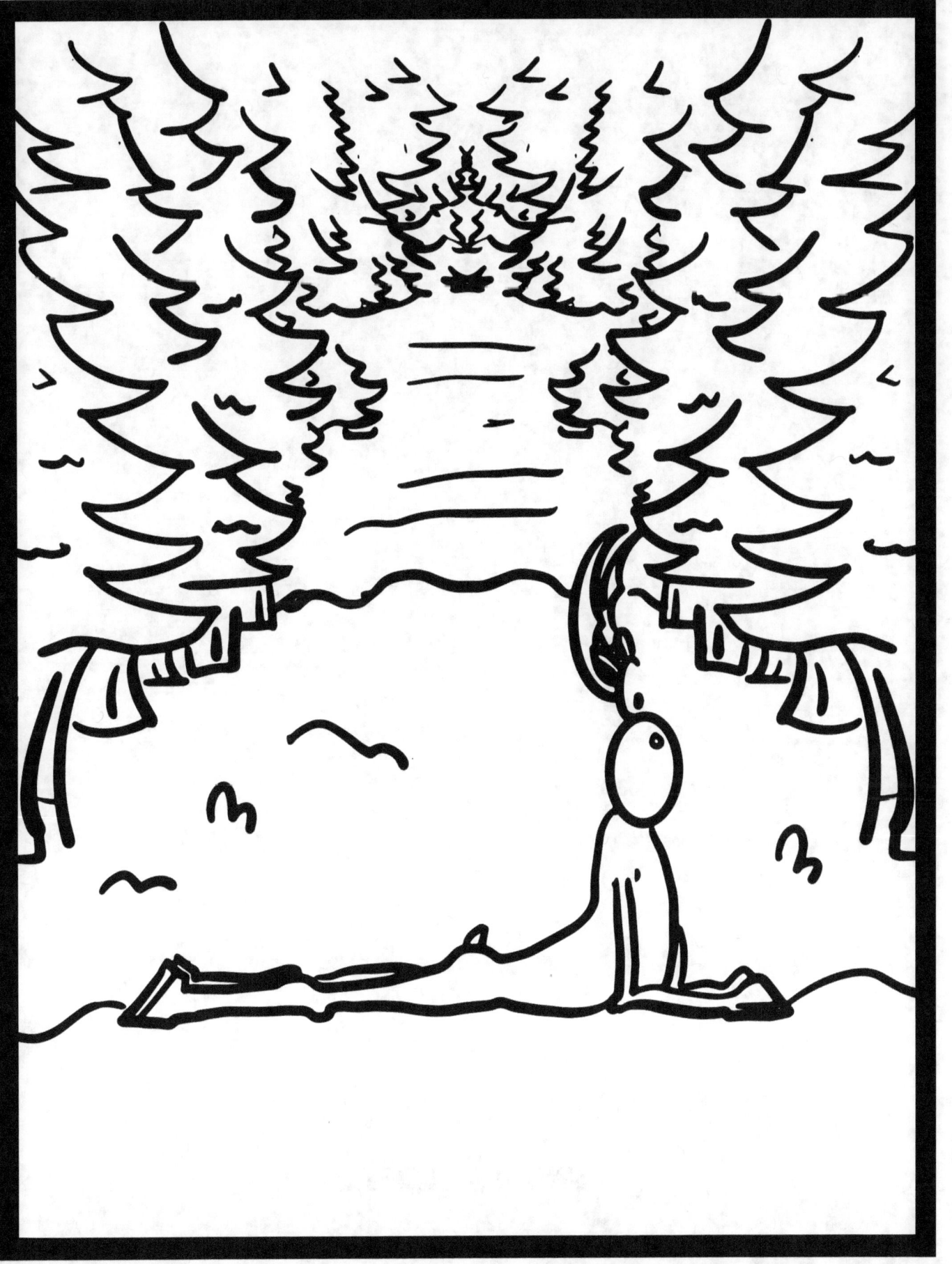

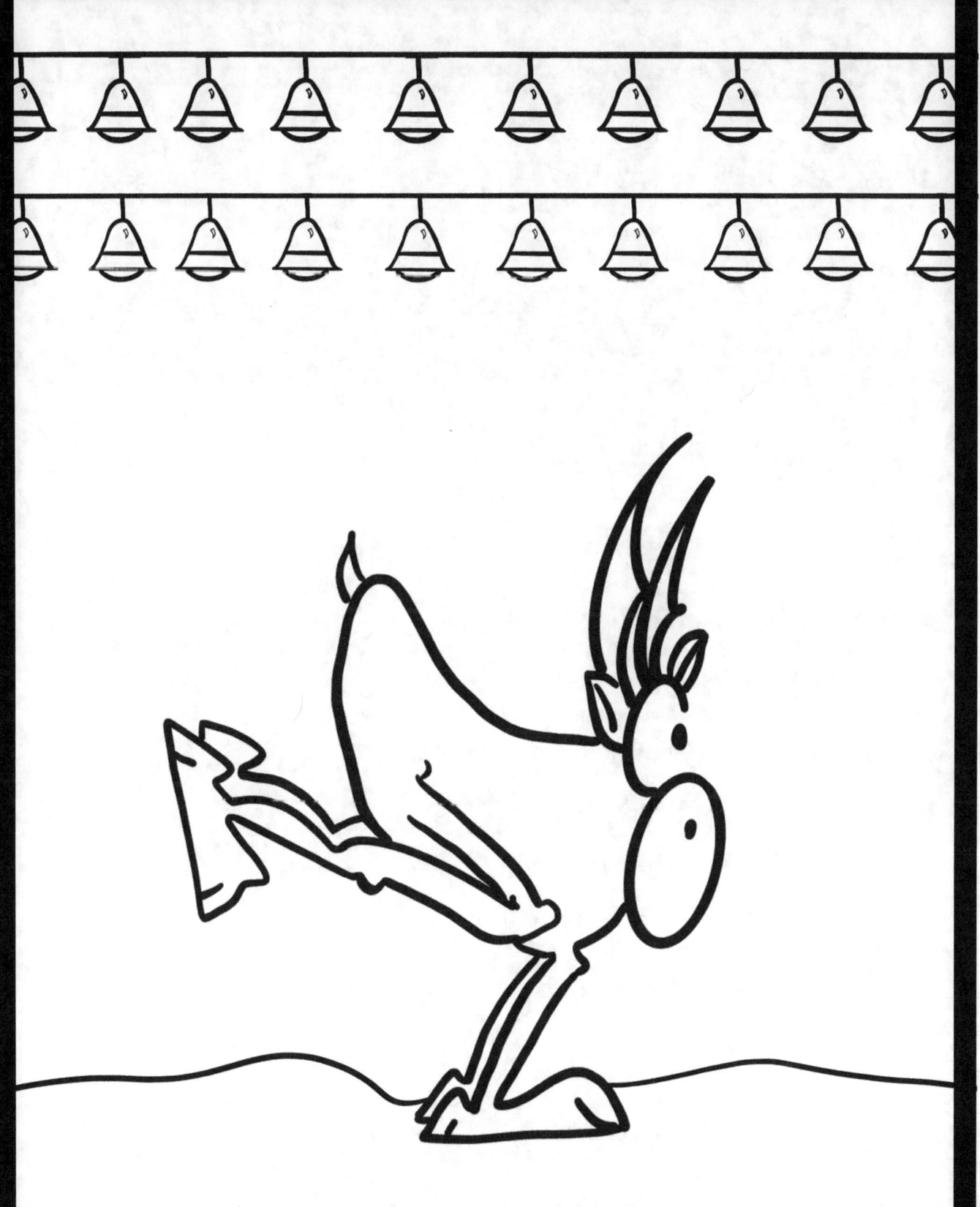

CROW-BELL REINDEER

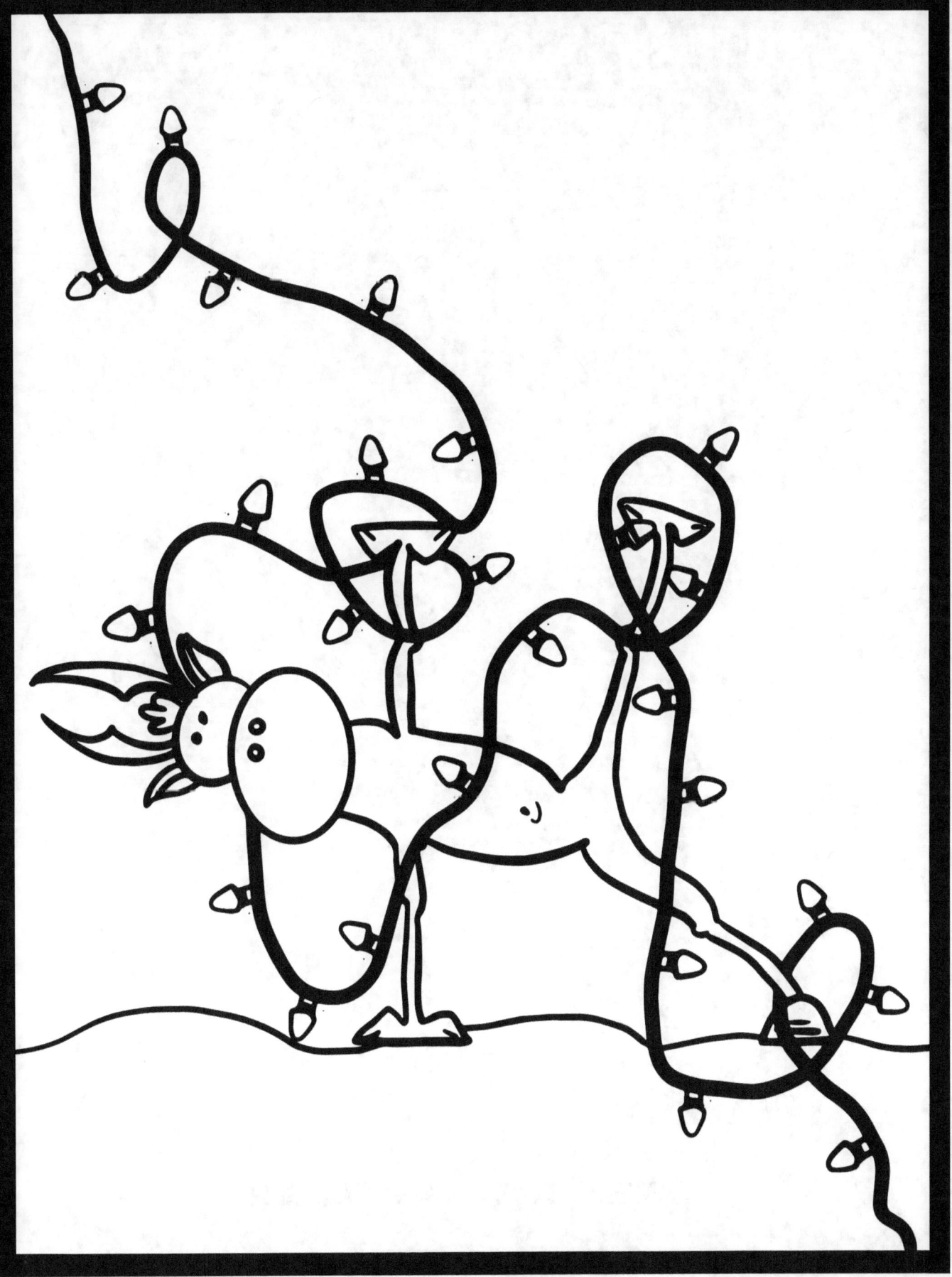

TANGLED SIDE ANGLE REINDEER

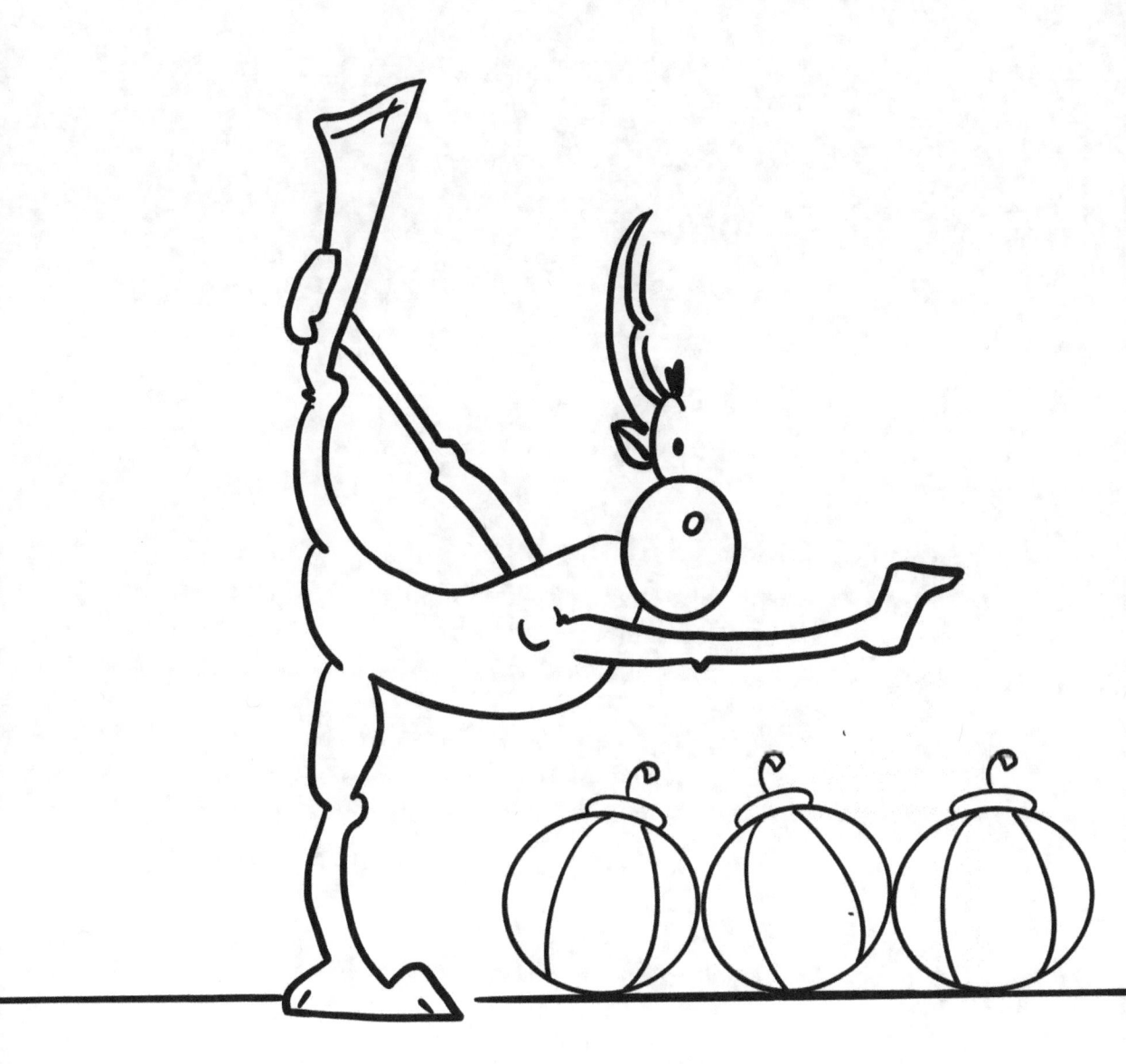

GRACEFUL DANCER REINDEER

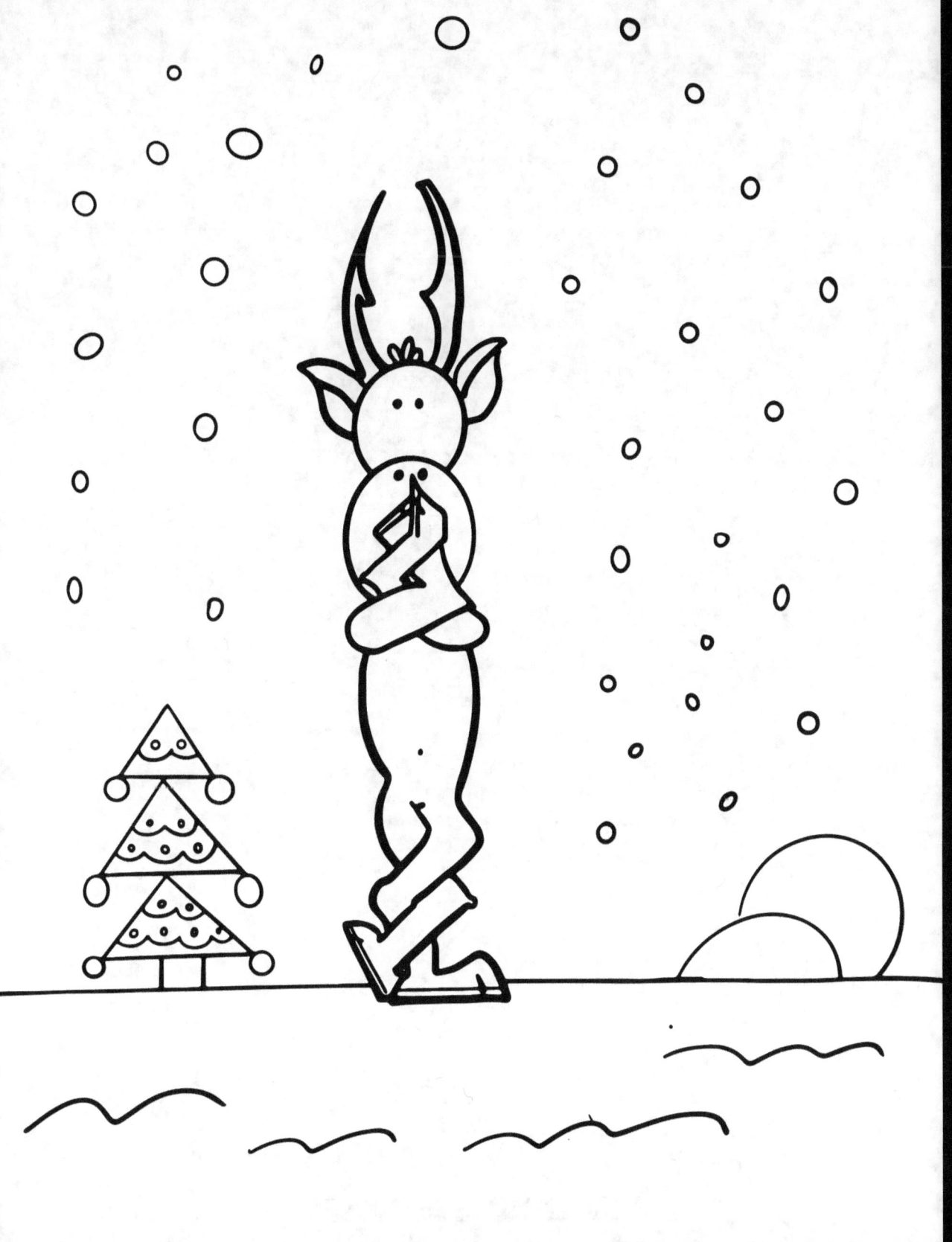

EAGLE POSE REINDEER

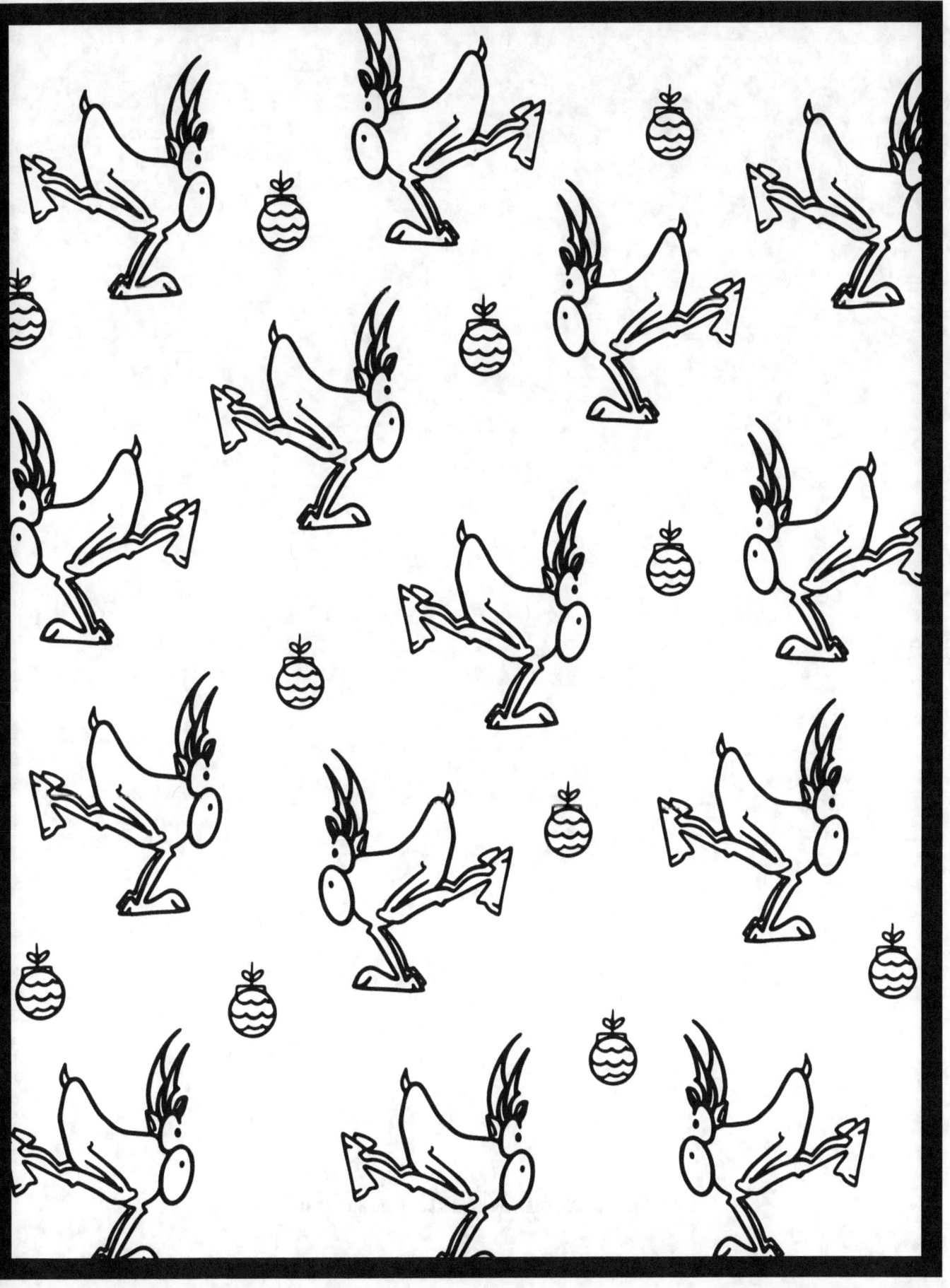

CROW REINDEER PATTERN

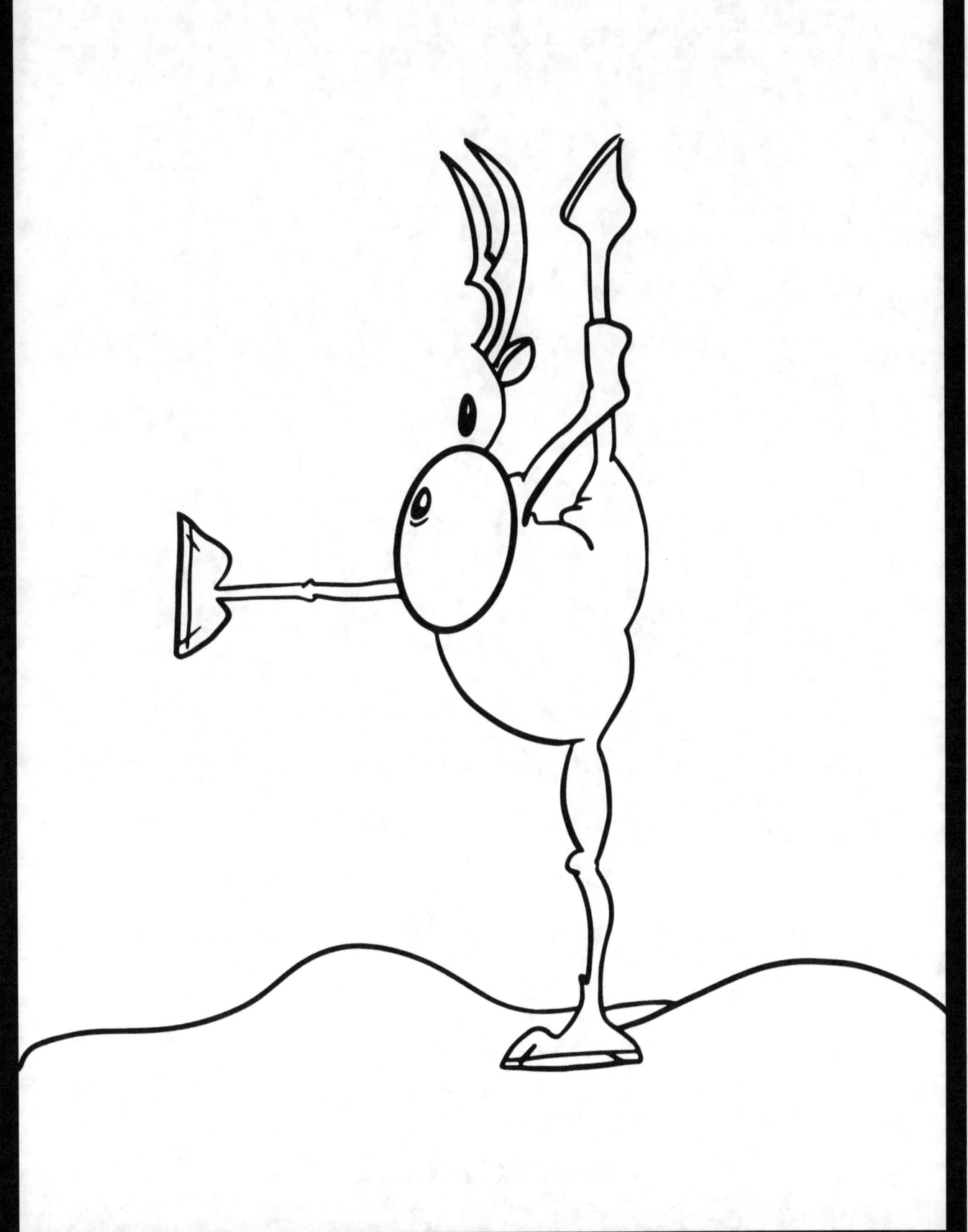

DANCER REINDEER

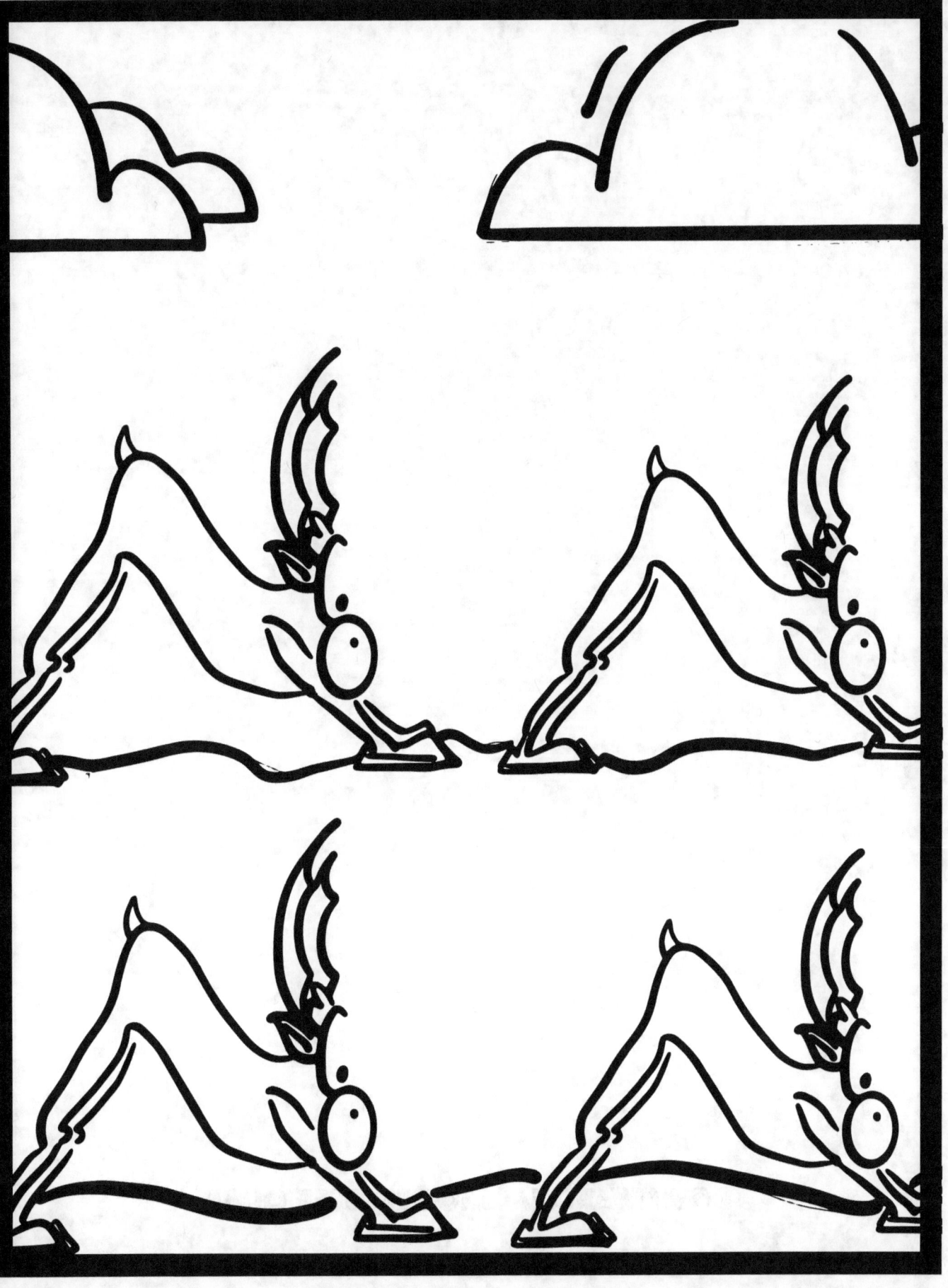

DOWNWARD FACING REINDEER QUAD

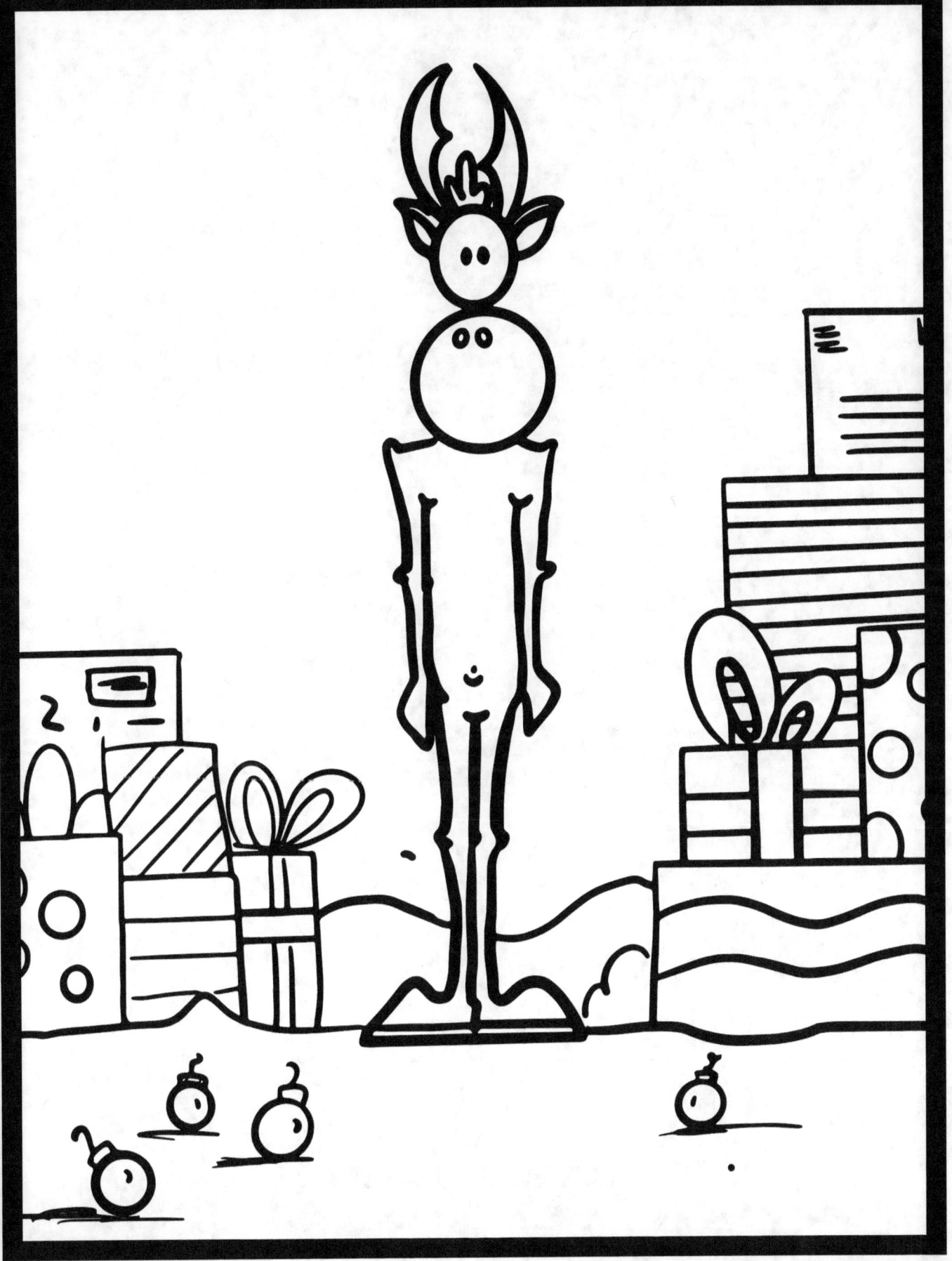

MOUNTAIN REINDEER

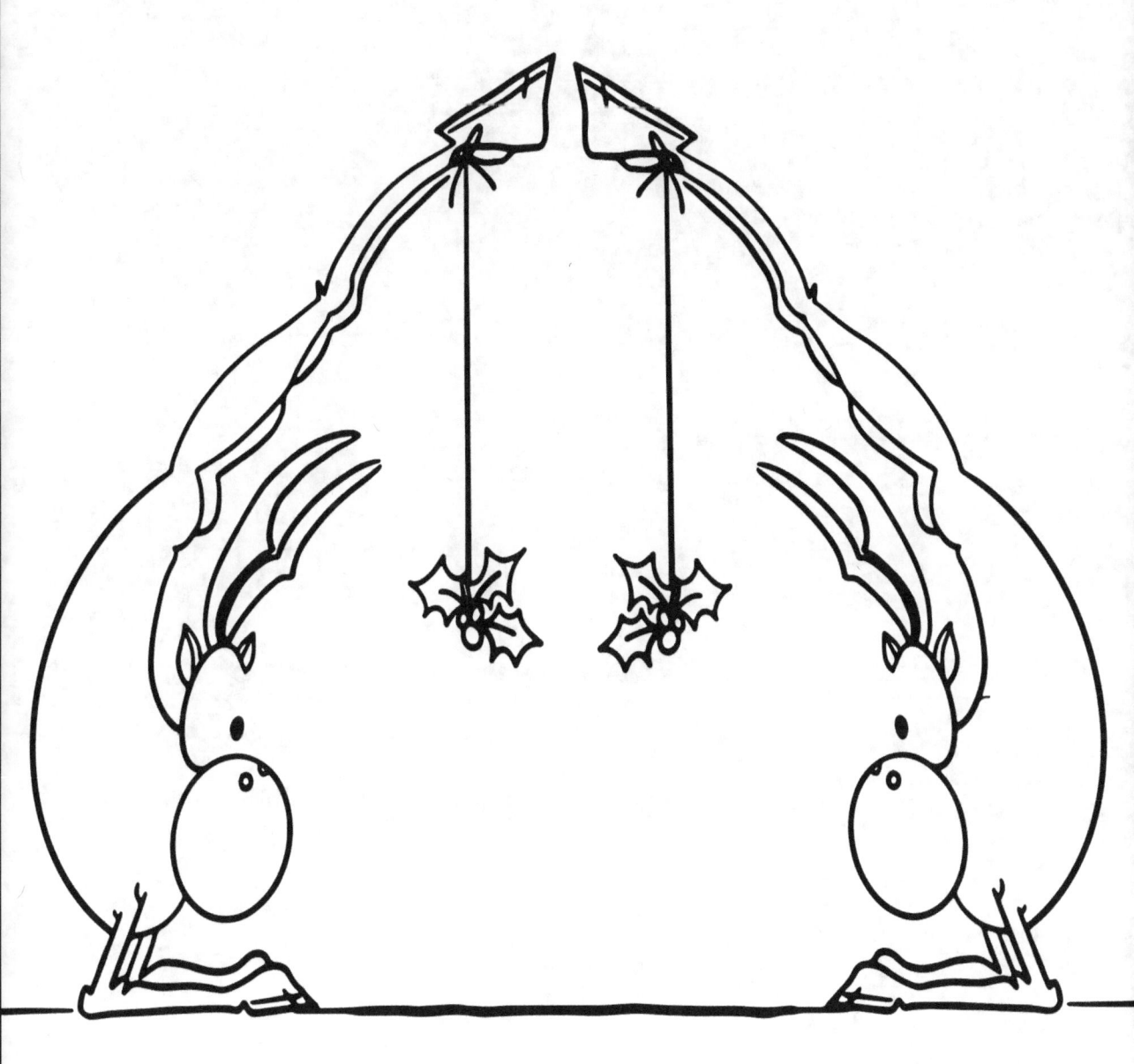

DOUBLE FOREARM STAND REINDEER

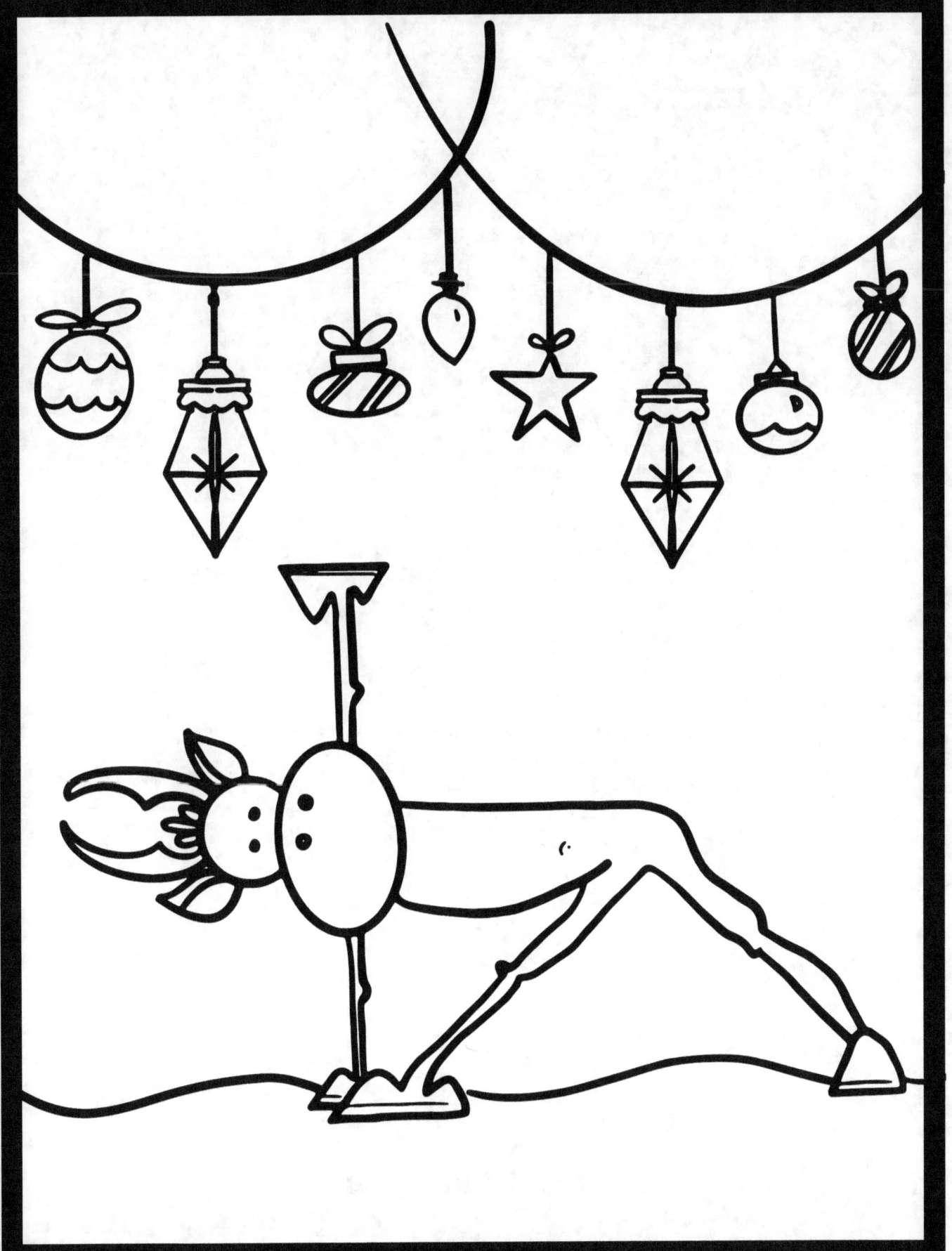

TRIANGLE REINDEER

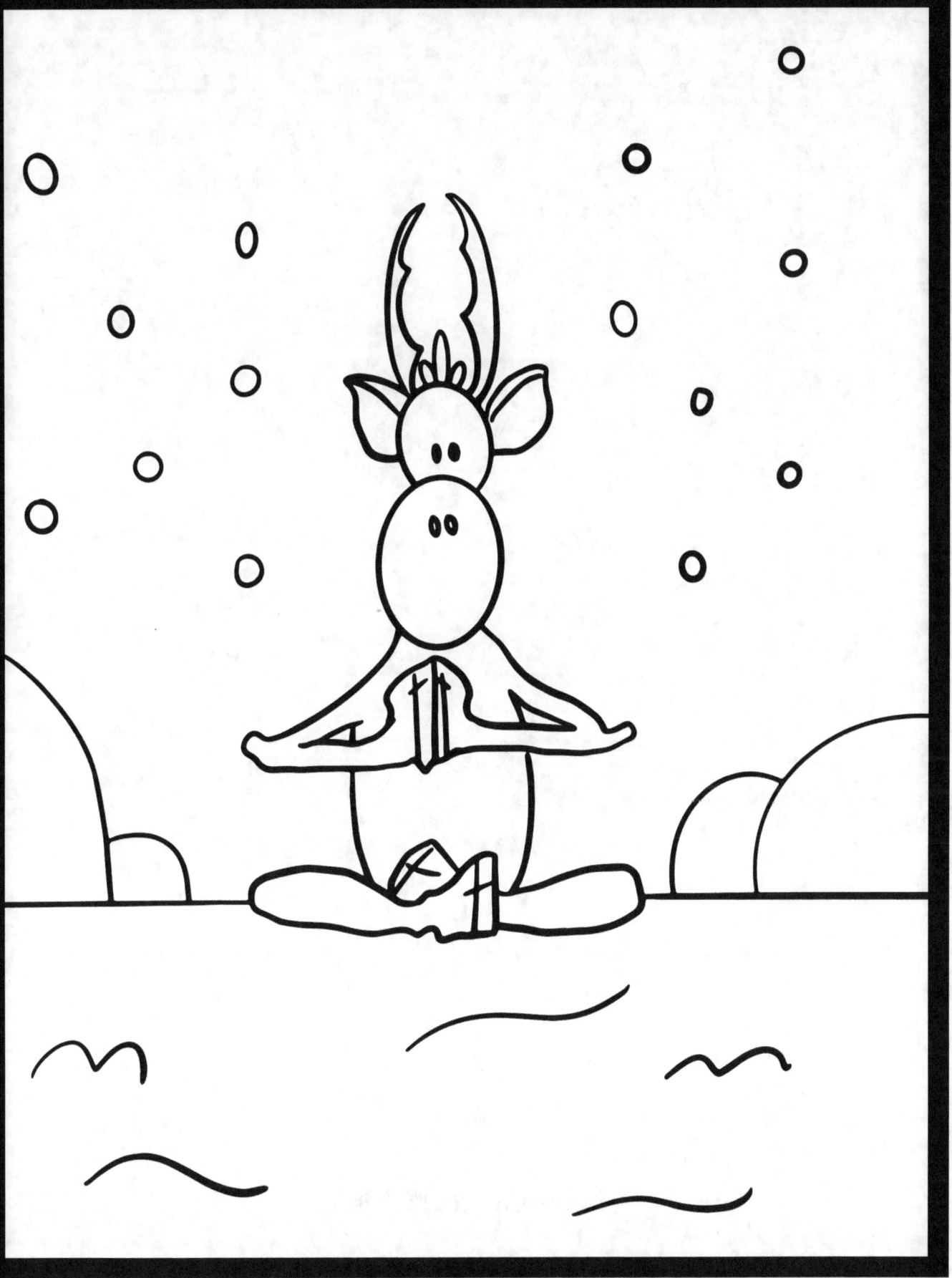

www.ingramcontent.com/pod-product-compliance
Lightning Source LLC
Chambersburg PA
CBHW081419220526

45467CB00009B/2751